Book Title:

Getting to Know Your Farrier: A guide for the horse owner.

THANK YOU FOR YOUR
PURCHASE...We hope you enjoy this book.
If this book contains any print errors, contact
customer service for a free replacement copy.
We are dedicated to providing you a quality product
for an affordable price.

Disclaimer:

As with all horse related activities, all techniques suggested in this
guide are to be approached with caution since horses can be
unpredictable and may have different reactions. It is always a good
idea to consult a professional/ specialist if you are unsure about any
of the aforementioned exercises. The author will not be responsible
for, nor will accept any liability for any injury or loss incurred.

Copyright ©2012 Bryan S. Farcus

All rights reserved.

ISBN# 978-0-9858241-2-9

Published by:

FARRIER-FRIENDLY™ SERVICES

Athens, OH 45701

Website: www.farrierfriendly.com
Email: farrierfriendly@hotmail.com

Book cover: photos and illustrations by Bryan S.Farcus

Table of Contents:

Preface :

It was the late 1980's when I first entertained the thought of becoming a professional horseman. At that time, I was just finishing up my bachelors' degree in accounting and I was not as excited as my peers to enter the "concrete jungle".   I was convinced that the reason for my lack of interest in working in the business community, as an accountant, was the inevitability of dealing with the stress of being around business managers or account supervisors with all their problems on a daily basis.

For some people, me being one, I couldn't face the idea of being chained to a career that I would regret.   It was at that point that I had what I thought was a great epiphany; I'm still young, why not make a change.   I could go to school, become a professional horse trainer or farrier—problem solved.   I could be in the *horse* business.   I would work with horses, not people, avoiding all of those worries!

Well, not quite.   Twenty-five years later and I must admit, though I have no regrets, I did have a real awakening.   It wasn't long into my new career that I realized that I was actually into more of a *people* business and the horses that I desired to work with would be "reachable" only if I was successful in all aspects of a business.   It became obvious that I would face many of the same challenges— managing finances and dealing with certain stressful situations of others, just as I had feared when considering a career as an accountant.

I now know that a successful farrier must be somewhat of a "jack-of-all trades". During the course of a farrier's professional life, he/she will be asked to *wear many hats.*

The farrier business is, undoubtedly, one of the few truly free enterprises that still remain in America. It is our (the farrier's), obligation to make sure that we maintain balance, not only for the feet of our horses, but also in the daily interactions that we have, as we attempt to offer the best possible service to all those concerned horse owners.

I hope that this guide will give you more insight into the world of your farrier. Often times, just knowing a little more about where someone has come from will help you both get to where it is you would like to go.

Thank you for your interest in *"Farrier-Friendly"*™ and good luck as you continue your journey of learning with your horse *and your farrier.*

Your friend in horses,

Bryan Farcus MA,CJF-BWFA

All too often we, as a people of a faster, more subservient life style, tend to lose sight of who the people around us are and what they are really about. In general, I believe that we tend to fixate on the immediate tasks at hand and we simply take for granted the great preparation that is required to offer what might appear to be a simple and straight-forth service. For instance, we rarely reflect on how our global communication systems work. Whether it is in the primitive form of telephones and the postal service, or the most modern versions of communication, such as satellite images, cell phones or "tweets", there exist hidden components that are essential in keeping these services alive for our random access. It is of no great surprise that a similar "behind the scenes" network exists in our

horse world, as well. Often, it is your farrier that is a liaison between you, your horse, and the industry that surrounds you.

Due to a growing demand for horses in the recreational setting, it is increasingly important for horse owners, as well as any horse professional, to be exposed to a solid foundation of knowledge that can be built upon. In this day and age, your farrier carries an awesome responsibility. He/she must, not only cope with all the immediate surroundings posed them (i.e. the manual task of trimming/shoeing a particular horse, customer concerns and any workplace obstacles), but there are also some overlooked aspects that must be dealt with. Many intangibles, such as liability, taxation, product development, and purchasing/marketing skills, tend to be overlooked.

Most people see their farrier as solely a craftsman and fail to see the other *hats* he/she must wear from time to time—a business person, educator, technician, and *yes,* maybe even a psychologist at times.

A Mission to Follow...

Even though farriers of our country are of a free enterprise system and practice without any government control, they have imposed some ethical regulations among themselves. These guidelines include a clear mission in an attempt to maintain quality control for all the horses and people that they might serve.

The mission of a reputable farrier is a simple one and should coincide with the generally accepted mission that was originally set forth upon the creation of the *American Farrier's Association.* :

"To further the professional development of farriers, to provide leadership and resources for the benefit of the farrier industry, and to improve the welfare of the horse through continuing farrier education."

A good farrier is kind to your horse and courteous to you, but no farrier can be the farrier you desire without your help. Here are a few tips to help you develop and maintain the best possible working relationship with your farrier:

❶ Plan your farrier visit on a day that you are not in a hurry.

❷ Pick a work area for shoeing that is large enough to safely work in...
   ☑ A good rule of thumb... If the area is big enough to comfortably stand two horses, then it is big enough to shoe one.

❸ Have your horse in from the pasture and ready...
   ☑ A brushed horse with clean picked hooves always makes for a more positive experience.

❹ Spend the time necessary to get your horse gentle to the touch of his body/legs, before attempting to pick up feet ...
   ☑ A respectful horse is a happier horse—Be the leader, so he can find comfort in you.
   ☑ Practice moving him into a light-footed posture.
   ☑ Practice picking-up the lighter foot.

❺ Get in the habit of noticing what is special about your horse's hooves:
   ☑ Don't be reluctant to ask any questions of

curiosity, a good farrier will encourage it.

    ☑ Also give your farrier a complete history of your horse, both physical and behavioral. Each time a farrier works on a horse he/she is put at risk. This is not the time for a *"don't ask, don't tell"* approach.

❻ Your farrier will appreciate the professional courtesy of notifying him/her no later than 24hrs. in advance of cancelling an appointment:

    ☑ And yes! ... a good farrier should return that courtesy. In this age of cell phones and texting, it's much easier for a farrier to let you know if he/she is running late.

    ☑ Finally, find out ahead of time what terms of payment your farrier prefers. A hard working farrier will appreciate you as a valued client and be able to focus all his/her energy on the needs of your horse.

When it comes to you and the relationship between your farrier, I urge you to examine what might seem obvious, try to pick-up on what might not always be said, and never leave your questions open for an opportunity that may mislead you. A new and revitalized relationship with your farrier can be one that will grow stronger for years to come. And, in turn, become something that both, you and your horse, can count on.

A Farrier's World:

Horse Behaviors

Customer Relations

Hoof Anatomy

Business & Tax Concerns

Hoof Physiology

Hoof Care Products

Horsemanship Safety Zones

Shoe Shaping, Leveling & Fitting

Tools

Safe Nail Approach

Measuring & Trimming

A Farrier's World

Horseshoe Nails

Hoof Health

Horseshoe Types

Conformation Assessment

The many "Hats" your farrier will wear on any given day...

▶ A Business planner.

▶ A Communicator/ Educator:

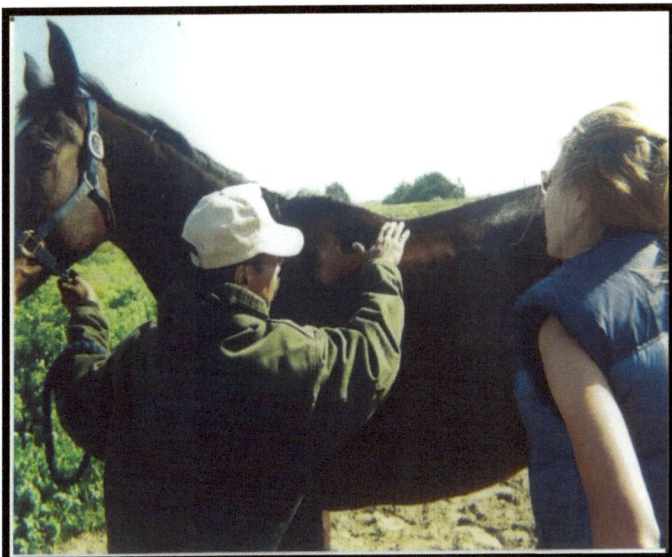

Photo by King Lamadora

▶ Liaison between Veterinarian &Horseowner:

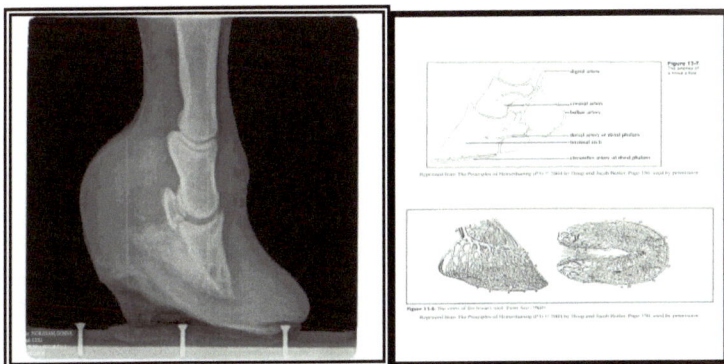

▶ *A Horsemanship expert:*

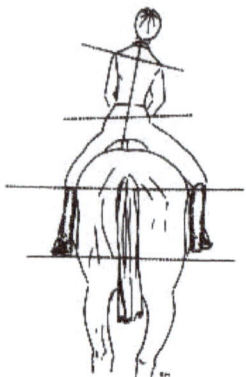

Photo courtesy of Jessica &Noah Fox

▶ *A Craftsman:*

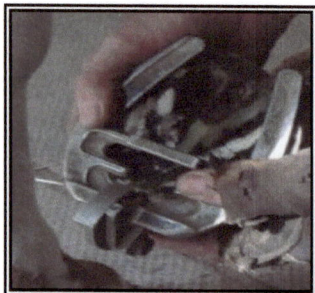

Photos by Bryan Farcus

▶ *A Lameness expert:*

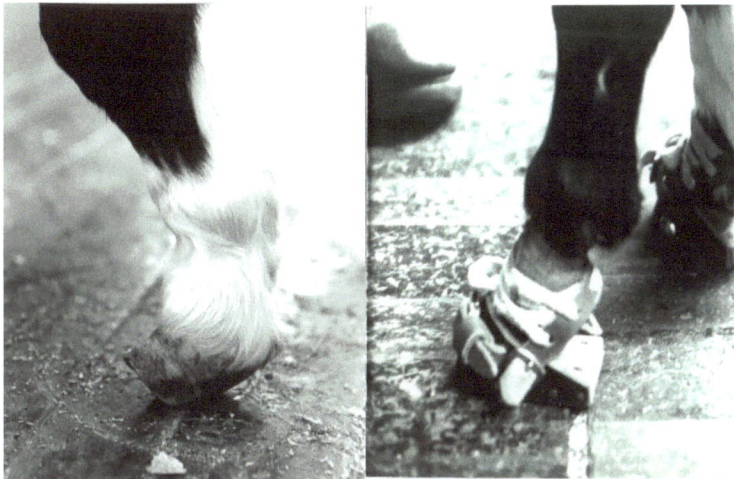

Photos by Bryan Farcus, CJF

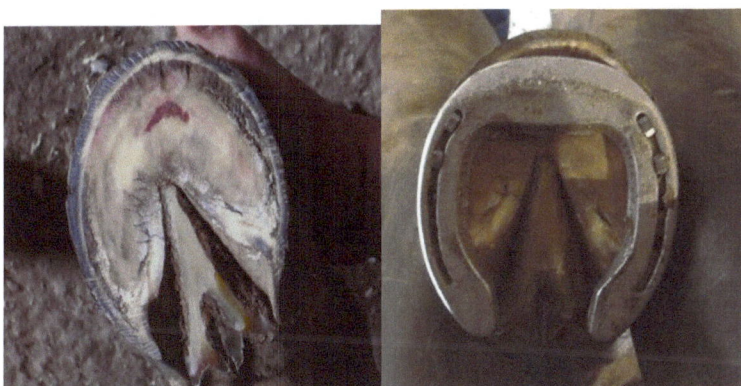

Photos by Kirk Underschultz, CJF

Helpful Tables & Graphics:

This page is reprinted with permission from the
Author of
HORSE FOOT CARE
By Dr. Doug Butler

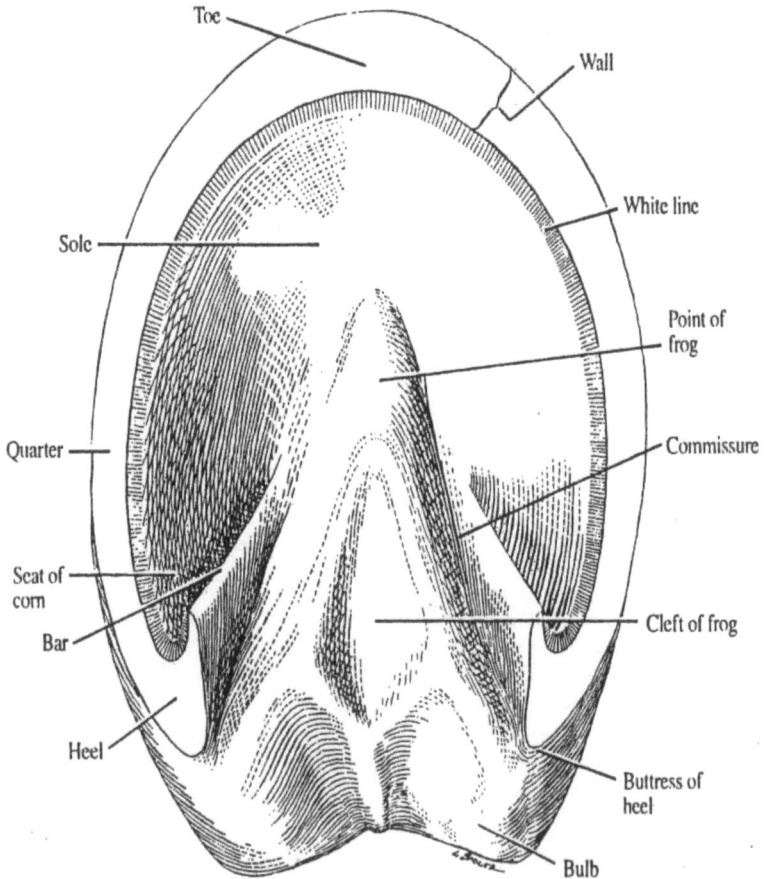

Toe
Wall
White line
Sole
Point of frog
Quarter
Commissure
Seat of corn
Cleft of frog
Bar
Heel
Buttress of heel
Bulb

The parts of the hoof

Figure#2:

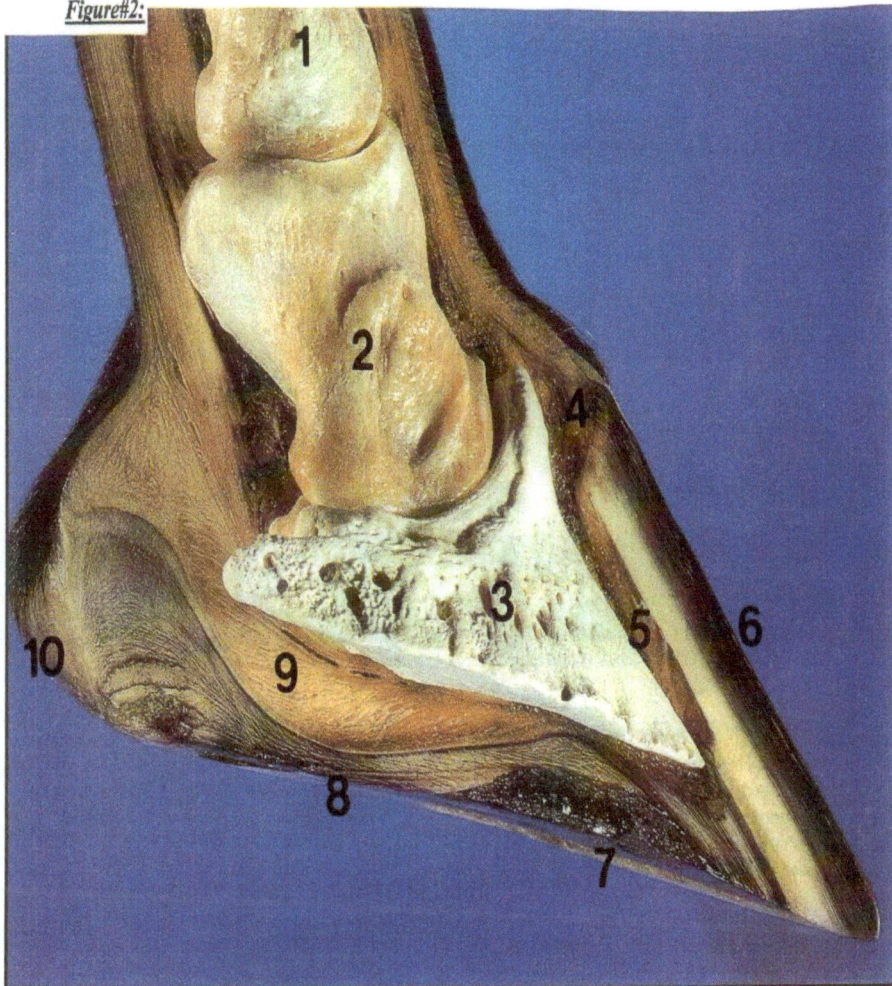

LATERAL OBLIQUE VIEW OF EQUINE DIGIT. Soft tissue is removed from one side of the phalanges.
Used by permission, courtesy of : The American Farriers Journal, ©1999 Lessiter Publications, Inc.

1. First Phalanx (long pastern).
2. Second Phalanx (short pastern).
3. Third Phalanx (coffin bone).
4. Coronary Band.
5. Sensitive Laminae.
6. Hoof wall (toe region).
7. Sole.
8. Frog.
9. Deep Digital Cushion.
10. Bulb of foot.

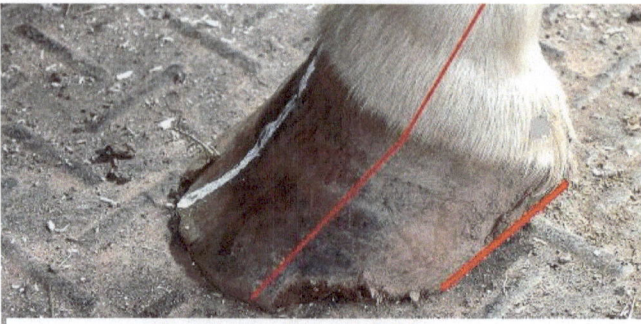

Broken-Back Axis

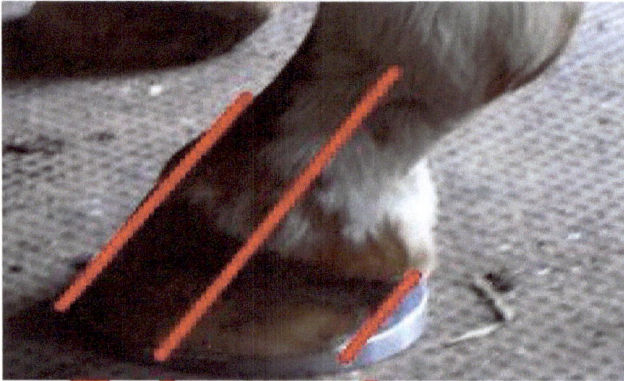

Balanced

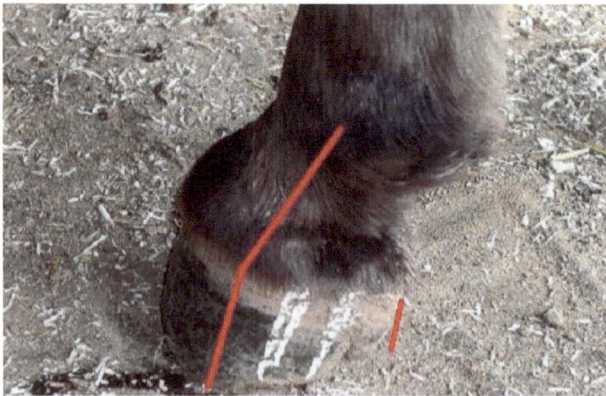

Broken-Forward Axis

Photos by: Bryan Farcus CJF

Glossary of Terms:

Axis BB (Broken-Back): hoof to pastern digit axis line that is visualized to represent a long toe/low heel hoof conformation.

Axis BF (Broken-Forward): hoof to pastern digit axis line that is visualized to represent a short toe/high heel hoof conformation.

Bars: viewed from the bottom of the hoof, minor protrusions present on both sides of the frog, a connective tissue that ties the buttress of the heel to the sole, acts to reinforce the heels.

Bar shoe: general term used to indicate any shoe that is closed or connected at the ends to maximize weight bearing surface, often used to stabilize a weak hoof or support a weakness in a limb.

BBLS: (Basic Body Language System) a term used to identify any system of communicating with the horse through herd instincts, based on predetermined gestures, signals, or cues that are horse logical.

Bulb: located at the back of a hoof connecting the frog and the coronary band, often referred to as the frog band.

Glossary of Terms [continued] :

Buttress of Heel: the part of the hoof wall that runs to the open end of the foot, often referred to as the point or butt of the heel.

Conformation: an overall view of the horse's entire body, comparing the horse's body structure for symmetry and/or functional alignment.

Commissures: the grooves that are present on either side of the frog, sometimes referenced as the paracuneal sulci.

Corrective shoeing: an approach to shoeing with a major emphasis on changing the horse's stance and/or way of going.

Coronary Band: a band of soft tissue that surrounds the top of each hoof nearest the hairline.

Club footed: a hoof that grows excessively high in the heel as compared to the toe length, there are various degrees of severity, generally considered "clubby" if the horse's hoof-to-pastern is broken-forward, due to a flexor tendon contracture that is extreme enough to distend the coffin joint.

Glossary of Terms [continued] :

This condition may be due to an injury, but most commonly inherited.

Deep Digital Cushion: also know as the plantar cushion, a fibro-fatty tissue underlying the frog that functions as a shock absorber.

Degree Pad: wedged shaped pads that are placed between the hoof and the shoe that will raise the hoof and lift the rear surface of a limb.

Deviation: a departure from a predetermined ideal, a term often used in horse conformation analysis to describe crookedness in a limb.

Dynamic Hoof Balance: evaluation of hoof balance as it pertains to the horse in motion, considering how the hoof will land and load.

Frog: a triangular shaped, elastic pad-like tissue that is located at the bottom of the foot that acts to absorb concussion and aid in traction

Gait: a pattern of movement or the way in which the horse travels, certain gaits are natural to all horses but some can be artificial.

Glossary of Terms [continued] :

Hoof Anatomy: the study of the structure/parts of a hoof.

Hoof Physiology: the study of the function of a hoof.

Interfering: a term used to describe the hitting together of a horse's foot to an opposing limb in a manner that restricts the horse's ability to move forward in a comfortable manner.

Keratination: a process whereby the division of horn producing cells accumulate to produce outer layers of hoof wall to protect sensitive tissue, similar to our own nail growth.

LLD (Limb Length Disparity): a condition where the horse suffers from a structural difference of his limbs as a working pair, often a curvature of the spine and/or a clubbed footed conformation is present.

Low-Underrun Heels: When viewed from the side, the heels of the horse are collapsed and low to the ground, the slope or angle of the heel is much lower than that of the toe.

Glossary of Terms [continued] :

Phalanx -1st : the first bone in the lower limb directly below the fetlock, also known as the long pastern.

Phalanx -2nd: the second bone in the lower limb directly below the fetlock, also known as the short pastern.

Phalanx -3rd: the third and last bone in the lower limb directly below the fetlock, also known as the coffin bone.

Quarter: when viewed from the bottom of the hoof, the region of hoof wall that is between the toe and heel.

Sensitive Laminae: an interlocking, velcro-like tissue within a hoof that is responsible for connecting the hoof wall to the coffin bone.

Seat of corn: viewed from the bottom of the hoof, a junction where the edge of the bar, sole and white-line come together, an area susceptible to attracting debris that can result in a sore spot (corn).

Sole: the flat, ground surface portion of the hoof, responsible for creating a natural pad that is designed to protect the coffin bone.

Glossary of Terms [continued] :

Static Hoof Balance: a view of hoof balance when the horse is at a stand still, using a geometric reference (X,Y,Z planes) for a three dimensional perspective.

Supportive Shoeing: fitting a shoe with enough length and width to protect and support the entire limb.

Therapeutic Shoeing: an approach to shoeing that provides a level of comfort and also attempts to remedy a hoof disease.

Vertical Depth Tolerance: a general reference to the amount of exfoliated sole that is able to be safely trimmed without causing the horse to be tender.

White line: usually yellowish or brown, it is the connective tissue (terminal ends of the sensitive laminea) that bonds the hoof wall to the sole, aids in nail placement.

Resources & Recommending Reading :

RESOURCES...

American Farrier's Journal , Lessiter Publications

Shoeing In Your Right Mind , Dr. Doug Butler

Six Figure Shoeing , Dr. Doug Butler

WEBSITES...

www.butlerprofessionalfarrierschool.com

www.myhorsematters.com

www.horseshoes.com

ASSOCATIONS...

AAPF, American Association of Professional Farriers,
www.professionalfarriers.com

AFA, American Farrier's Association,
www.americanfarriers.org

BWFA, Brotherhood of Working Farriers,
www.bwfa.net

About The Author :

Bryan S. Farcus MA, CJF-*BWFA* ~

For the past 25 years, Bryan has been combining the skills of horseshoeing, teaching, and riding. He is a Certified Journeyman Farrier through the Brotherhood of Working Farriers Association (BWFA) and also holds a certification in Equine Massage Therapy. Bryan's other accomplishments include both a Master of Arts degree with a specialization in equine education and a Bachelor of Science degree in the area of business.

For more than ten years, Bryan was the director/ instructor of a Farrier Studies program at an international equestrian college and a guest instructor for others, as well.

These days, he continues his teaching by offering various "horsemanship for horseshoeing" programs. Upon invitation, Bryan presents demonstrations and group discussions on basic hoof care and horsemanship, in order to promote the advancement of equine education. Bryan is also the creator of a select line of "*Farrier-Friendly*™" products and currently authors a series of "*Farrier-Friendly*™" articles that appear in horse magazines throughout the US. Bryan currently works with horses and their owners in Ohio and West Virginia. You can visit him at:

www.farrierfriendly.com or e-mail: farrierfriendly@hotmail.com

www.ingramcontent.com/pod-product-compliance
Lightning Source LLC
Chambersburg PA
CBHW041756050426
42443CB00023B/22